EXTREME
SKATEBOARDING

Philip Wolny

rosen publishing's
rosen central ®

New York

Published in 2020 by The Rosen Publishing Group, Inc.
29 East 21st Street, New York, NY 10010

Copyright © 2020 by The Rosen Publishing Group, Inc.

First Edition

Library of Congress Cataloging-in-Publication Data

Names: Wolny, Philip, author.
Title: Extreme skateboarding / Philip Wolny.
Description: First edition. | New York : Rosen Publishing, 2020. | Series: Extreme sports and
stunts | Audience: Grades 5–8. | Includes bibliographical references and index.
Identifiers: LCCN 2019011136| ISBN 9781725347496 (library bound) |
ISBN 9781725347489 (paperback)
Subjects: LCSH: Skateboarding—Juvenile literature. | Extreme sports—Juvenile literature.
Classification: LCC GV859.8 .W65 2020 | DDC 796.22—dc23
LC record available at https://lccn.loc.gov/2019011136

Manufactured in the United States of America

Disclaimer: Do not attempt this sport without wearing proper
safety gear and taking safety precautions.

CONTENTS

INTRODUCTION   4

CHAPTER ONE
SKATING TO THE EXTREME   6

CHAPTER TWO
GETTING INTO GEAR   14

CHAPTER THREE
STEPPING ONBOARD   21

CHAPTER FOUR
SKATING SMART, SKATING SAFE   27

CHAPTER FIVE
SUPERSTAR SHREDDERS   32

GLOSSARY   39
FOR MORE INFORMATION   41
FOR FURTHER READING   43
BIBLIOGRAPHY   44
INDEX   46

INTRODUCTION

Skateboarders live to ride and love to push boundaries. A great pro can make it look easy and natural. In reality, all skaters put in hours upon hours of practice to nail each trick. This is true for everyone, from the highest-paid skater on the circuit to the beginner who is too nervous to leave their driveway before they start going to the skate park. Anyone can skate, and it is possible to skate pretty much anywhere that is paved.

The most extreme tricks and maneuvers can look nearly impossible to pull off when you're just starting out. However, remember that every skater has gone through the same journey as you and your friends. Everyone has to start at the bottom and work his or her way up. For a beginner, even an ollie can feel like an extreme trick when you land it for the first time. This feeling of accomplishment is part of the lure of skateboarding.

The sport has come a long way since it was a side project for surfers for when the waves were not very cooperative. Skateboarding shares some similarities with surfing and snowboarding, but in many ways it is truly a sport like no other. It is one of the most individual of sports. Even in competitions with others, you are your biggest competition. Building on a simple move, like an ollie, adding layers to one's skating game, and slowly getting better over time are all

Skateboarding often attracts thrill seekers—those who are going for the fastest, longest, highest, and most difficult tricks and maneuvers. For many, skating is more than a sport—it is a lifestyle.

exciting aspects of skateboarding. Gear up, hit the street or park, and find out more about the extreme world and sport of skateboarding.

CHAPTER ONE

SKATING TO THE EXTREME

Few sports inspire the passion and dedication that skateboarding does. Skating is enormously popular in North America and around the world and supports a multibillion-dollar business and culture. Professional skaters can make good livings in the sport, while some of its biggest names, like Tony Hawk and Bob Burnquist, have carved out fortunes from their love for skating and extreme sports.

"SIDEWALK SURFING"

Many people agree that skateboarding first arose on the West Coast of the United States, specifically California, and derived from surfing. When it first began, it was practiced only by a small group in one part of the world, unlike the global phenomenon it is today.

Surfing was first developed by Hawaiians and other Polynesian peoples long ago and was imported to Southern California. When the California waves did not allow for surfing, handy surfers took roller skates and attached them to wooden boards. Others performed similar modifications with children's scooters by taking away the steering post or simply removing the wheels to glue or nail them onto a separate wooden board.

Some people initially called skateboarding "sidewalk surfing." This new do-it-yourself (DIY) hobby became wildly popular. It got so big that the Roller Derby Skate Company, formed in La Mirada, California, produced a commercial skateboard in 1959. At that point, skating was on the map and would never truly go away.

In the mid-1960s, Hobie, Makaha, and other surfboard producers began manufacturing their own skateboards. The first real skate contest was held in Hermosa Beach, California, in 1963, in the yard of Pier Avenue Junior High School. Orange County, of which Hermosa Beach is part, was a hotbed of surfing and surf culture, too. Pop and rock duo Jan and Dean even released a 1964 hit music single entitled "Sidewalk Surfin'."

ROLLING WITH THE Z-BOYS

Around ten years later, about 20 miles (32 kilometers) north of Hermosa, a crew of skaters often gathered at the Zephyr Skate Shop in Santa Monica. Santa Monica and neighboring Venice Beach became known worldwide for this still-new and exciting sport. The popularity of skating had faded a bit since the 1960s. Many cities and towns nationwide had banned it. Police, teachers, and government officials lined up against skating, declaring it dangerous and even antisocial.

Skate legend and entrepreneur Stacy Peralta poses with the film poster at the 2001 premiere of *Dogtown and Z-Boys*, the skating documentary he directed.

The Z-Boys, including future skating star Bob Biniak, got their name from the Zephyr shop. They had a reputation for being troublemakers and misfits—a reputation they liked and sometimes even promoted to others. The Z-Boys pioneered a skating style that resembled surfing in some ways, but the moves were done on streets, sidewalks, and other concrete surfaces. Media coverage, word of mouth, and companies that formed to build better and varied boards for different kinds of skating helped grow the sport.

POOLS, PARKS, AND STREETS

You might know the expression, "If life gives you lemons, make lemonade." As a true DIY sport, skating often changes and reacts to unforeseen circumstances and transforms. For example, an early 1970s drought in California pressed lawmakers to ban having swimming pools filled up much of the time. This setback for homeowners proved to be an opportunity for young skaters: they found they could practice new and exciting tricks in empty pools. Pool skating spread to other parts of the world but really took off in skating's birthplace of California.

By the end of the 1970s, some towns and businesses had begun to open actual skate parks, designed with obstacles and other elements for skaters to use. Several hundred existed throughout North America by 1980. For a long time, however, many skaters did what they had learned to do best: improvise. They skated in abandoned construction sites, out-of-the-way reservoirs, ditches, and other such destinations where they could practice their tricks and test their skills.

A SPORT GROWS ... AND TAKES FLIGHT

Skater Alan Gelfand made extreme sports history when he developed the ollie in 1978. Pioneers like Rodney Mullen would take the ollie and other tricks to invent—and then revolutionize—street skating. Street skating, rather than using pools, ramps, or other special environments, uses the streets and other public spaces. Slides, grinds, and other tricks are performed with whatever is available.

Freestyle skating is similar to street skating but concentrates on doing tricks mostly on flat ground. For a time, many freestyle skaters had carefully choreographed routines, including music. Eventually, freestyle was absorbed more or less into street skating.

The 1980s saw another skating revival. This time, the founding of magazines like *Thrasher* (launched in 1982) and *Transworld Skateboarding* (1983) helped spread skating—and skater culture—all around the world. Street skating, and skateboarding generally,

The event logo is displayed at the ESPN X Games 15, held in 2009 in Los Angeles, California. The annual festival was partly responsible for a skating revival.

REINVENTING THE (SKATE) WHEEL

One major development in skateboarding was the invention of urethane wheels. Frank Nasworthy, a surfing enthusiast, recalled a visit to a plastics factory where they were experimenting with polyurethane used in roller skate wheels. With some experimentation, he produced wheels like these for a skateboard. While old wheels—like the metal ones borrowed from roller skates—were metal or clay, these new ones provided a smoother, quieter ride with better grip.

At first, Nasworthy sold the wheels personally to surf shops and other buyers. He even placed an advertisement in some surfing publications featuring a young legend of the sport: Gregg Weaver. As his company, Cadillac Wheels, grew bigger, he licensed his product to established skateboard manufacturers and inspired other companies to compete and make their own. Many people think these new wheels really helped blow up the sport in the 1970s as much as any other factor.

continued to be viewed by adults with a "get off my lawn" mentality, although "get off my street" might be a more appropriate description.

Skaters started their own companies. Meanwhile, styles such as vert skateboarding (short for vertical ramp skating) exploded in popularity. The X Games competition was launched in 1995 to feature extreme sports, including skateboarding. In the years since, skating styles have continued to branch out, with young women joining the sport more than ever. Men dominated the sport in the early years.

SKATING TODAY

At the most basic level, skateboarding is fun. The cost is very low, too. A decent board, helmet, and pads are the only required gear. Skating takes strength, agility, and endurance—but you do not need any of these at the level of a world-class athlete to begin skating. You merely need to work at it, slowly but surely. Those who put in the time to practice every day eventually see results, even if they can barely balance on the deck of a skateboard at the beginning. Today, there are several categories of skateboarding and each has its own following, both in the United States and around the world:

Freestyle: This may be the oldest distinct style of skating. Tricks and moves are done on flat ground, on outdoor concrete or similar surfaces. As skateboarding grew in popularity in the 1960s and 1970s, skaters devised choreographed routines set to music to better impress onlookers.

Street: Arising partly out of freestyle, this type of skating, as its name implies, is performed on sidewalks, curbs, and streets, using structures as obstacles on which to do a variety of ollies, slides, and grinds. Common obstacles include walls, benches, tables, stairs, railings, and more. Rodney Mullen and other street skaters popularized and helped drive the development of this style. Mullen was the first to do an ollie on flat ground. That basic skill—launching the board into the air and then landing back on the board— opened the door to countless other tricks and techniques.

Vert: This style is performed on ramps and other structures with vertical inclines, such as bowls or pools.

Zach Miller of the Adio Street Skate Team catches some air off a vertical ramp at a shopping mall in September 2007, in Orange, California. This kind of skating is extremely popular.

Moving from the bottom or lower area up the ramp provides the motion needed for various tricks. Vert skating especially makes use of aerials, since one of the main goals of many vert moves is to catch air: launch oneself high up past the lip, or edge, of the ramp or other structure.

Park: This style incorporates elements of street and vert. Many parks have half- or quarter-pipe structures, pools or pool-like formations, and street-style obstacles and courses.

Downhill/slalom: Downhill styles of skateboarding can be done for pleasure, or in competition, and concentrate more on a limited set of techniques. Such styles often stress speed and finishing a race in first place.

CHAPTER TWO

GETTING INTO GEAR

F ew things are as nerve-racking as getting on that skateboard for the first time. But the first step is to get a skateboard. You can find one online easily enough from hundreds of reputable sellers. However, as a first-timer, you might want to check out boards in person. That way, you can gauge their weight, feel, and other characteristics.

Skate shops are probably the best places for beginners to pick out boards and safety equipment. A skate shop sells skateboarding gear and accessories exclusively. Many sporting goods stores also sell boards and skating accessories, but skate shop employees are experienced and knowledgeable, likely more so than chain sporting goods store employees. Do not be afraid to ask questions—every skater was a beginner at one point.

Shop staff are often active skaters themselves. They can be a great resource to find out about events, competitions, new tricks, trends, deals, and more. Most important, they will help you pick a board that is right for your size, experience, and needs. You can buy a board that is ready to ride or ask the shop to help put one together for you.

A BOARD FOR ALL SEASONS

All boards are set up the same way. The deck is the main wooden piece of the skateboard that the skater stands on.

The opposite ends of the board are curved upward, with the front part known as the nose. The other end is the tail. Most decks are screwed into base plates in two places (front and back). These base plates connect to the trucks, which are the pieces holding the wheels to the deck. The trucks can turn in the direction in which you lean while skating, allowing you to control the direction of the board and execute other motions.

Are you going to be doing tricks with your new gear? If so, you will want a short board that is between about 28 and 32 inches (71 to 81 centimeters) long.

There is no real trick to starting skating. You simply have to get on the board and do your best. Finding your balance and comfort level is key.

TAKING A FALL THE RIGHT WAY

Losing control of the board is common. It will happen to you over and over again as a beginner. If you do fall—and you will—avoid the natural instinct of reaching out with your hands to brace for impact. Instead, for falls where you are obviously going to hit the ground (known as eating dirt), pros advise to tuck in the elbows to one's chest and make the effort to roll onto your shoulders or back. You can practice falling like this by getting on your board on soft grass or a similarly soft surface and then intentionally falling forward into a roll. Keep your limbs loose, because tightening them makes bone breaks and fractures more likely. Exercise caution and wear your protective gear, even when you practice.

One popular standard size is about 31 inches (78.7 cm) long and 8 inches (20 cm) wide.

Shorter boards are less stable, but easier to control. Longer boards are typically harder to control than short ones, but are more stable. Meanwhile, a board's wheels affect performance, too. If you want to be able to go faster, pick hard wheels that are bigger. Small and soft ones allow for more tricks and easier turning.

A board that is too wide takes too much energy to move or do tricks on, while one that's too narrow will be unstable and hard to balance on. Skaters over 5 feet 3 inches (160 cm) tall—meaning many teens and adult riders—will want a board that is at least 7.5 inches (19 cm) wide.

WHAT'S OUT THERE?

For most kinds of skating, especially street and park, a standard or "Popsicle" deck is the most common type because of its functionality. It is so named because it is shaped like a Popsicle stick. The nose and tail of a Popsicle board are nearly symmetrical.

For simply cruising around town, a cruiser skateboard is a strong option. Cruisers have kicktails and, according to the online skate shop Tactics, "are ideal for getting around because they are lighter and more nimble than larger longboards." They come in a variety of shapes, while standard boards are all the same Popsicle stick shape.

For long rides, and especially for downhill skating, longboards are your best bet. Tactics notes, "longboards are often 8 to 12 inches (20–30.5 cm) longer than a standard skateboard … [and are] highly customizable for many types of riding." One kind of longboard skating is slalom. Like the type of skiing it is named after, slalom involves downhill skating around and between carefully placed obstacles, usually traffic cones.

A longboard should be specifically suited to the needs of the kind of skating you are doing. Consulting with an expert at a skate shop can really help you find the right fit.

Big, soft wheels give slalom longboards extra traction. The truck and wheel assembly might be positioned or constructed differently on certain kinds of downhill boards depending on the type of performance the skater is looking for.

For a blast from the past, you can also try out old-school style skateboards, also known as shaped decks. These are often wider than 8.25 inches (21 cm) and are a style once commonly used for pool, vert, and bowl riding in decades past.

TRUCKS AND WHEELS

Which wheels and trucks will best meet your needs? Trucks come in three general sizes: low, mid, and high, which match the distance from the hanger of the truck to the deck itself. Low-level trucks provide more stability for certain tricks. Mid-level trucks are considered all-purpose for most skaters, and, according to Warehouse Skateboards, an online skate shop, "are solid choices for park or street skateboarding." High-level trucks are good for big wheels and are ideal for cruising and carving, especially with longboards.

TO CLOTHE AND PROTECT

Skating is a physical sport, with risk of injuries both great and small. Trying to look cool by avoiding helmets or pads can backfire spectacularly. It can lead to many very uncool things: an injury that sidelines you from skating for weeks or months, or one that lands you in the hospital with debilitating injuries, including brain damage from head trauma—or even death. So make sure you always wear a helmet. While a helmet protects the skater's head, elbow pads, kneepads, and wrist guards protect those important areas.

It is worthwhile to invest in some good skate shoes if you can afford them. You might even be able to find some secondhand without too much wear on them. Skate

Not any shoe will do for a serious skater. Skate shoes, like Vans, are specifically designed to handle the rigors of riding and performing tricks.

shoes are designed to provide the best grip on the soles to do tricks with, padding on the sides, and, often, extra cushioning to absorb the impact of landings and other movement. Skate shoes or sneakers should provide maximum comfort and mobility. Anything heavier or thicker will make skating tough.

Most skaters use grip tape on their boards. This tape is sticky on the side facing the deck and very rough on the side facing the rider, like sandpaper. Well-designed shoes and grip tape work together to keep you from slipping off your deck.

CHAPTER THREE

STEPPING ONBOARD

The time has come! If you have never gotten on a board before, this is what you have been waiting for. Make sure to warm up with some stretches and put on your helmet and pads.

Before hitting a skate park, it might be a good idea to get a little practice in by yourself, even with other beginners. Some people learn better on their own, while others need competition or company to push themselves.

TAKING IT TO THE STREET

The street is generally where newbies first try skating. On the sidewalk, or on any paved surfaces, always remember: safety first. A split-second mistake can mean getting hit by a car or seriously injuring a pedestrian. Learn the rules of traffic and abide by them if you need to use the street. However, as a newcomer to skating, you should find a nearby park, plaza, or other out-of-the-way or little-used space.

THE RIGHT STANCE

Tactics skate shop recommends a tried-and-true test to determine which foot is best to put forward. Ask a fellow skater to gently nudge you while you stand on the ground. As you make the effort to catch your fall or stumble, notice which foot you use first to brace yourself. That will usually be the correct foot to put forward. Someone who rides with his or her left foot at the front of the board and pushes with his or her right foot rides in what is called a regular stance. The opposite stance (right foot on board, left pushing) is called riding goofy. These names arose years ago and are merely part of the skate lingo, so you should not consider them derogatory or insulting.

Use grass or another soft surface to your advantage to get comfortable with being on a board. Place your foot on the board. That first foot should face the front, or nose. When you are feeling confident, push off with the other foot and bring it behind the other. Your

You may need a bit of help with your stance when you first start out. Know your limits, ask for help, and have fun.

front foot should be near the front of the board, over the front trucks, the rear foot toward the back and over the rear trucks. Anyone coming into skateboarding from surfing or snowboarding will find her or his stance more natural than other beginners.

MAKING MOVES

Now, when you are ready to skate for real, get into position on a sidewalk or other paved surface where you can move around safely. With both feet on the board, your feet should be positioned across the width of the board, above the trucks. Now, push off. As you start moving, bring your pushing foot back onto the board. Ride around a bit and get comfortable.

Now try turning. Shift your weight back on your heels, and the board should turn in the direction your back is facing. You just did a frontside turn! Putting pressure or weight on your toes while leaning toward the front of the board is the exact opposite, called a backside turn. For now, get used to being on the board, turning, and cruising.

The style of skating you are interested in will dictate your journey from beginner to seasoned veteran. However, it makes sense to master cruising, turning, and simple tricks first, before getting ambitious and tackling vert skating. Do not get ahead of yourself, because that is the road to certain injury. In addition, expecting too much out of yourself too soon will only frustrate you and discourage you from pursuing the sport. Take your time and you will enjoy yourself much more—and you will also reduce your risk of injury.

GETTING VERTICAL

If riding pools or bowls or vert skating on half-pipes and quarter-pipes is more your cup of tea, it is recommended that you first learn some of the street skating basics already mentioned. In skating, you generally build new tricks on top of simpler ones. The ollie is a component of many other moves that followed it, for example. Before trying vert, make sure you have mastered a few basic flips, grinds, and other moves.

The fun starts at the bottom of the vert ramp. Step onto your board and push up one of the sides of the pipe. You will push up until you start to lose speed and cannot really push anymore. Just as you start to roll back down, push your wheels downward against the ramp with your legs. Roll back, and try it again and again. This is called pumping, and it is how you maintain and gain speed on a ramp. Practice is key. Before you know it, you will have made it to the top of the ramp.

In vert skating, the moment of truth is dropping in for the first time off the lip of a ramp or other structure—the only way is down! Beginner skaters should not try this because it is possible to really hurt yourself if you do not have a lot of experience on a board.

BEGINNING TRICKS

The first set of tricks most skaters learn are flips and grinds, but this is only after getting comfortable cruising and turning. Here are the most common beginner tricks to learn, in order of difficulty, with basic explanations.

- **Kickturn**: Some people consider this to be the most fundamental simple trick. When a skater needs to execute a quick turn, Steve Cave of ThoughtCo says, "instead of simply leaning and carving, you lift your front trucks off the ground, and pivot." He recommends mastering it first, even ahead of the ollie and other basic moves.

- **Ollie**: This is one of the most basic and important maneuvers for a skater. Standing on the board, push down hard on the tail of the board with the back foot. As the tail is hitting the ground and the front of the board is lifting, lift your front foot up with it and jump in the air. This should all take place almost simultaneously. While you and the board are airborne, level out the front foot and bring it to the board's front. Then land flat on all four wheels. It takes a little practice to get the timing right.

A skate park is one of the best places to get some skating in, regardless of one's skill level.

- **180 ollie**: This is a more advanced trick, but it is basically the ollie with a 180-degree turn incorporated. Begin similarly to how you would with an ollie. Bend down and twist your shoulders a bit in the direction you are going to turn to prepare to move your body into the 180-degree motion. Pop the board, pushing the back tail with the foot to make the turn, trying to control the turn's direction with the front. This can be done either frontside (turning in the direction your back is facing) or backside (in the direction your front is facing).

- **Kickflip**: Braille Skateboarding says, "Although the kickflip is one of the most basic skateboarding tricks, it's also one of the most [...] difficult to master." This trick begins with an ollie, starting with the ball of your rear foot placed on the tail of the board, and the front resting just behind the bolts, facing forward at about a 45-degree angle. In mid-ollie, lift your front foot as you would in a regular ollie. Instead of getting it to the nose, however, move your foot to the back edge of the board to flip it. The board should do one rotation and come back to its original position for your landing.

CHAPTER FOUR

SKATING SMART, SKATING SAFE

A head of everything else, one rule you need to follow in skateboarding is safety first. Always do your best to land new tricks, but do not push yourself unnecessarily. Skating can be competitive. Of course, being obsessed with any sport or activity can be unhealthy, especially to the exclusion of everything else. Remember to always keep skateboarding about fun.

A LONG WAY DOWN

Nobody should underestimate the dangers of injury from skating, especially from high-flying ramp skating. It is not just the height, but the speed achieved on a ramp or other structure that can give a skater's body a great deal of power as it shoots through the air. Steve Cave, an online journalist writing about skateboarding on ThoughtCo, points out how inadvisable it is to complain about wearing pads and skip it altogether: "If you are uncomfortable with all those pads on, remember this—you will be riding on wooden slabs screwed together. Sometimes, the screws work themselves a little

The higher you go, the longer you have to come down if you are not careful. Be aware of your surroundings at all times when skating.

loose and stick up just a little. Now, imagine yourself falling off your board, and sliding on your knees, and finding that screw. Would you rather it take your knee pad off, or your knee cap? I suggest you choose, 'pad'!"

PROTECT YOUR HEAD

Serious head trauma can lead not only to permanent brain injury but can even prove fatal. You should always wear a helmet that sits low on your forehead, has V-shaped side straps that sit around the ears, as well as a tight-fastening and secure buckle. Ensure that you can put two fingers (and no more) between the strap and your chin.

The helmet should be padded within and should fit on the rider's head snugly. A snug fit means it does not move around if you shake your head. It should also not interfere with any other movements or in any way impair your hearing and vision. Check periodically to make sure your helmet is still in good condition and has not cracked, has not lost any of its padding, and the strap has not weakened. Helmets need to be replaced about every five years or so.

Besides making sure your safety gear—like your helmet and pads—is in good working order, check every time you skate that

Modern helmets are sleek, comfortable, and essential, whether you are a pro or just starting out. Wearing one ensures you can have years of safe skating ahead of you.

your boards and all its component parts are all secure and screwed in properly. If you have not ridden in a while, your trucks might get loose or rusty, depending on where your board is stored.

SOME TIPS FOR STAYING SAFE

Like other sports, skateboarding requires you to warm up and stretch before you go out on your board. A good warm-up should get your blood moving and your body ready to go.

Stay relaxed and loose. That will keep your muscles and limbs from being prone to injury from falling. If you do feel yourself falling, try to crouch low to reduce the height you fall from, and thus your impact.

Keep your eyes peeled and concentrate on where you are going.

Besides your safety gear, make sure to wear weather-appropriate clothing while skateboarding. You do not want to overheat or get too cold.

Avoid riding in the street—at all, if possible. Obey any and all local laws that apply to skateboarding. Also do not ride your board into or along large crowds of pedestrians, as it is a recipe for collisions and minor accidents.

Be respectful of pedestrians, drivers, and others in public. While the "outlaw" image of some skaters can be appealing, keeping things polite and legal is a win-win for everyone involved.

RISK VERSUS REWARD

Many skaters' instincts are to always reach for the next and most daring maneuver, to prove their skills to themselves and their friends. For example, you might see a skater in competition ollie up very high onto a railing for a great grind, or hurtle down a big staircase. All of these tricks are risky and dangerous and take many painful falls to master. When you see these tricks in videos, you often see only the

It may seem extreme and sophisticated when you first start out, but—with practice and determination—you will be doing rail slides like this in no time.

successful attempts and not the countless failed attempts and falls that were edited out.

Avoid feeling pressured to do daring and dangerous stunts. The greatest skaters do not need to prove their talent with daredevil tricks. Many of the best and hardest tricks are relatively safe. One example of a safe skater is Rodney Mullen. He is one of the most legendary skaters of all time, and he does nearly all his tricks on flat ground or small obstacles. You need not risk life and limb to be the best.

CHAPTER FIVE

SUPERSTAR SHREDDERS

P ractice makes perfect, and lots of practice is what it takes to become a really good skateboarder. You need talent, but, even more so, you need practice to become truly great. At the same time, most people will probably never become professional skaters. However, that should not stop anyone from admiring some of the veterans, innovators, and up-and-coming pioneers on the skateboarding scene today.

TONY HAWK: THE "BIRDMAN"

There are few people more important to skateboarding's history and development than Tony Hawk. He is a household name to generations of skaters. Hawk first got on a board in the late 1970s at age nine and started competing at eleven. Within a few short years, he was a member of one of skateboarding's most respected and exciting teams, the Bones Brigade, which was set up to help promote the Powell-Peralta skateboarding equipment and apparel company.

Hawk is an excellent all-around skater, but he mostly built his reputation doing vert tricks. Besides his skating, Hawk also started his own company, Birdhouse, to sell boards, clothes, and skate accessories. In addition, side ventures like his video game franchise, his work with various foundations, and his tireless efforts to promote skateboarding as a sport and culture have added to Hawk's reputation as one of the greatest skateboarders of all time.

One of Hawk's greatest claims to fame is inventing the 900, short for 900-degree aerial. This trick is done by gaining as much speed on the ramp as possible and then launching into an aerial with 2.5 revolutions (equal to 900 degrees). Hawk landed it on his eighth try at the 1999 X Games. He was the first ever to do the 900 and now many skaters have done so, following his lead.

Tony Hawk—shown here doing an aerial trick at a 2016 event in Canada—could well be the greatest legend in the world of skateboarding.

EXPLOSIVE STYLE: TONY "TNT" TRUJILLO

The Santa Rosa, California, native Tony Trujillo has carved out a reputation for himself with an aggressive style of skating that incorporates many old-school moves. As for many others, skating is more than a sport to him—it was also a lifestyle and culture.

Raised on a farm, Trujillo was seven when he first picked up the sport and took advantage of a neighbor's ramps to learn. He was good enough to win his first contest at age twelve, to get sponsored at fourteen, and to go fully professional at sixteen.

Trujillo's hardcore skating style matches many of his other interests—he likes extreme music like heavy metal and even plays in a rock band himself. Trujillo will sometimes skate in punk or metal style makeup. He skates fast and hard, and, according to Huckmag.com, with "an uncompromising style featuring a mastery of both street and transition."

RODNEY MULLEN: "THE GODFATHER OF STREET SKATING"

Alongside Tony Hawk, few skaters can claim to be as influential to the sport as Rodney Mullen. In 1983, Mullen came up with a trick originally called the magic flip and later renamed the kickflip. He earned the nickname "the Godfather of Street Skating" because his loose and easy style of street skating made him one of the best ever. Inventing tricks like the ollie impossible, Godzilla rail flip, the 540 shove-it, the double heelflip, and so many others cemented his reputation.

Mullen's career reads like a history of skateboarding itself. He won his first freestyle contest at just eleven years old, in 1977. He joined Powell-Peralta's Bones Brigade in 1980 and was later featured in several of their videos, one of the main ways of gaining fame and success as a

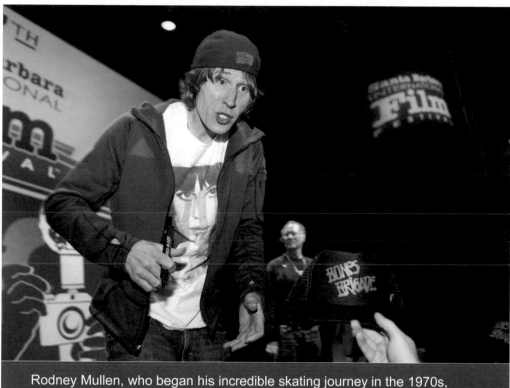

Rodney Mullen, who began his incredible skating journey in the 1970s, greets fans after a viewing of *Bones Brigade*, a 2012 Stacy Peralta film about the skate team he helped make famous.

skateboarder in that era. With fellow street skater Steve Rocco, Mullen launched the skate company World Industries, which saw great success. World Industries signed skaters to develop new brands and product lines and gave them a great deal of independence. The company gained a reputation for staying cool and authentic even as it grew bigger and bigger, a tough move in a sport where "selling out"—appearing to compromise yourself for financial or more mainstream success—is one of the biggest betrayals to hardcore skaters and skating enthusiasts.

CARA-BETH BURNSIDE: EXTREME RENAISSANCE WOMAN

In the 1990s, more women than ever before began skateboarding. This was before there were many major female skaters, and Cara-Beth Burnside certainly broke new ground. The California native has made a name for herself in both skating and snowboarding. She first skated at age ten and practiced six to seven hours at a time.

Burnside was the first woman to appear on the cover of *Thrasher* and also the first to have a signature skate shoe, released by Vans. More important than any of these firsts was going out there and doing her best in a male-dominated sport that was often declared too risky and challenging for women. To keep proving them wrong, Burnside founded Action Sports Alliance in 2005, a nonprofit association of female skateboarders and other extreme sports athletes.

She told *Vice* in 2018, "I just want to make cool things happen … If I can be the force behind helping other girls get to where they need to be—that makes me feel good." Part of that work is helping to get more prize money for female skaters at competitions and adding women's sports and categories in different competitions where they may have been lacking before.

NOW AND FUTURE STAR: LIZZIE ARMANTO

The Finnish-American Lizzie Armanto, from Santa Monica, California, put the world on notice with some impressive accomplishments at a tender age. Armanto specializes in bowl and vert skating and has won several dozen awards.

After she became famous, she was hired by the food company Kellogg's to feature her skating in a commercial for Cinnamon Frosted Flakes alongside the mascot Tony the Tiger. This was one of her favorite moments because she remembered being amused as a child by athletes endorsing her favorite cereal.

Armanto, even at the elite level at which she currently skates, still likes to spend hours mastering a new trick and will pay her dues to land it, like any other pro or dedicated amateur. She told the skate shop CCS.com in an interview how she always tried to hide her injuries from her mother as a teen skater. "[A]t the same time, I knew getting hurt was part of it. You had to learn how to fall, and I think that was a big key. But that doesn't stop you from falling. I am always falling."

Californian Lizzie Armanto dazzles audiences at Argentina's Xtreme Life Fest in September 2014, held in Buenos Aires.

TRY, TRY AGAIN

Like it or not, falling is a part of skateboarding. Get ready for it if you choose to dedicate your time and concentration to this exciting and ever-changing sport. Be ready for the scrapes, cuts, and bruises.

However, also look forward to getting better, feeling the rush of landing a difficult trick, and growing in the sport over

FAMOUS AND INCREDIBLE SKATE PARKS

Many skaters credit their love for the sport, and the skills they developed, partly with having a particularly favorite place to skate. Here are some of the best-known and dynamic skate parks around the world.

Burnside Skate Park: Situated under one end of Burnside Bridge in Portland, Oregon, Burnside was originally set up illegally by skaters themselves. Running the park remains a community-led effort and Burnside remains one of the world's most famous skate spots.

Louisville Extreme Park: Equipped with a 24-foot (7.3 m) full pipe, a street-skating area, transitions, and more, this park in Louisville, Kentucky, is open twenty-four hours a day and accessible for inline skaters and bikers, too. There is usually enough room for everyone in its 40,000 square foot (3,716 square meter) space.

The MegaRamp: Pro skater Bob Burnquist built this massive vert structure in Vista, California, to help himself and others practice. The MegaRamp itself is about 60 feet (18.3 m) tall and as wide as several football fields. The *San Diego Union-Tribune* described it as jaw-dropping, "like nothing you've ever seen in someone's backyard."

Denver Skatepark: This skate park in Denver, Colorado, has bowls "for every style and skill level, plus an extensive street course with ledges, hubbas, banks, and hips," according to Complex.com.

time. You will probably figure out within the first year or two whether you really have a talent and passion for skating and want to take things further. Even if you never get very good, remember that it was the fun you had along the way that matters most.

aerial Any airborne move that a skater executes off a ramp or similar structure.

base plate A rectangular piece of plastic that sits between a skateboard truck and a skateboard deck.

deck The wooden part of the skateboard on which the rider stands.

dropping in A maneuver in which a skater begins a ramp session by placing the tail or the trucks of a skateboard on the edge of the ramp and leaning in to the transition.

flip A basic skateboarding trick in which a skater turns his or her board over while in midair.

freestyle One of the oldest styles of skating, freestyle includes technical skating on flat surfaces.

grind A trick in which the rider moves the trucks of his or her board along the edge or top of an object, like a railing or sidewalk curb.

grip tape A strong, sticky tape applied to a skateboard to prevent slipping.

half-pipe A U-shaped ramp used to do aerial tricks.

hanger The lower part of a skateboard truck with the axle and wheels attached to it.

hubba The nickname for a wide swathe of concrete on either side of an outdoor staircase, upon which skaters often perform tricks.

nose The front of a skateboard.

ollie A basic jump in which a skater launches the skateboard straight up and lands back on it.

polyurethane A plastic-like material that is used to make wheels for skateboards, inline skates, and other wheeled products.

quarter-pipe Similar to a half-pipe, this kind of ramp has only a single transition. It is essentially one half of a half-pipe.

ramp A curved or inclined structure that skaters use to generate speed and height to pefrom aerial manuevers and other tricks.

slide A move in which the rider moves the bottom of her or his board along the edge or top of an object or obstacle.

street skating With its roots in freestyle, street skating is a genre of skating in which skaters do tricks while using urban obstacles such as stairs, sidewalk curbs, and other parts of the built environment.

trucks The metal assemblies that connect the board to the wheels.

vert Also known as transition skating, this style refers to tricks performed on half-pipes or in empty pools, in which the main goal is to get air.

Canada Skateboard
2337 Main Street
Vancouver, BC V5T 3C9
(604) 708-5678
Website: http://www.vsbc.ca
Twitter: @CanSkateboard
This Vancouver-based organization works to promote
    skateboarding throughout Canada. Its projects include
    helping refurbish skating facilities, including parks,
    working with community members, skaters, and
    local officials.

Harold Hunter Foundation
151 First Avenue
New York, NY 10003
Website: http://haroldhunter.org
Instagram: @haroldhunterfoundation
Twitter: @haroldhunter
YouTube: @HaroldHunterFdn
The Harold Hunter Foundation was established in the
    memory of iconic New York City skater and actor Harold
    Hunter. It is a grassroots, community-based organization
    that promotes skateboarding as a welcoming community
    and pursuit as an alternative to gangs and other
    negative activities.

Newline Skateparks, Inc.
6249 205th Street, Suite 101
Langley, BC V2Y 1N7
Canada
(604) 530-1114
http://www.newlineskateparks.com
Instagram: @newlineskateparks
Twitter: @newlineskate
New Line Skateparks is the longest-operating skate park
    design and construction team in Canada, with more than
    two hundred completed projects throughout North America.

Thrasher Magazine
1303 Underwood Avenue
San Francisco, CA 94124
(415) 822-3083
http://www.thrashermagazine.com
Instagram and Twitter: @thrashermag
Founded in 1981, *Thrasher* is one of the most respected
    and popular skateboarding magazines and provides a
    great jumping off point for riders new to the sport and
    scene. It sponsors numerous events annually.

FOR FURTHER READING

Adamson, Thomas K. *Skateboarding Street Style*. Minneapolis, MN: Bellwether Media, Inc., 2016.

Borden, Iain. *Skateboarding and the City: A Complete History*. London, England: Bloomsbury Publishing, 2019.

Bowman, Chris. *Vert Skateboarding*. Minneapolis, MN: Bellwether Media, Inc., 2016.

Cefrey, Holly. *Competitive Skateboarding*. New York, NY: Rosen Publishing, 2013.

Donner, Erica. *Skateboarding*. Minneapolis, MN: Jump!, 2017.

Fitzpatrick, Jim. *Skateboarding*. Vero Beach, FL: Rourke Educational Media, 2016.

Michalski, Pete, and Aaron Rosenberg. *Advanced Skateboarding*. New York, NY: Rosen Publishing, 2016.

Nelson, Kristen Rajczak. *Skateboarding*. New York, NY: Rosen Publishing, 2016.

Nixon, James. *Skateboarding*. London, UK: Franklin Watts, 2017.

Stecyk, C. R. III, and Glen E. Friedman. *DogTown: The Legend of the Z-Boys*. New York, NY: Akashic Books, 2019.

Whiting, Jim. *Skateboarding*. Mankato, MN: Creative Education, 2019.

BIBLIOGRAPHY

American Academy of Orthopaedic Surgeons.
"Skateboarding Safety." OrthoInfo. Retrieved February
27, 2019. https://orthoinfo.aaos.org/en/staying-healthy
/skateboarding-safety.

Badillo, Steve, and Doug Werner. *Skateboarding: Legendary
Tricks*. Huntingdon, UK: Tracks Publishing, 2008.

Beal, Becky. *Skateboarding: The Ultimate Guide* Westport,
CT: Greenwood Publishing, 2013.

Broadly. "Meet the Skate Icon who was the First Woman to
Grace the Cover of Thrasher Mag." May 31, 2018. https://
broadly.vice.com/en_us/article/mbk3wx/cara-beth
-burnside-the-first-woman-to-grace-the-cover-of
-thrasher-mag.

Cave, Steve. "Basic Skateboard Tricks." ThoughtCo,
December 31, 2017. https://www.thoughtco.com/basic
-skateboard-tricks-3002986.

Cave, Steve. "Vert Skateboarding Basics." ThoughtCo,
December 4, 2017. https://www.thoughtco.com
/vert-skateboarding-basics-3002985.

CCS. "Lizzie Armanto Interview." Retrieved February 20,
2018. https://shop.ccs.com/the_catalog/lizzie.

Complex. "25 Best Skateparks in America." August 7, 2013.
https://www.complex.com/sports/2013/08/25-best
-skateparks-america/jim-griffith.

Girls Skate Network. "Spotlight: Lizzie Armanto." January
29, 2011. http://girlsskatenetwork.com/2011/01/29
/spotlight-lizzie-armanto.

Kidz World. "Cara-Beth Burnside Biography." October 16,
2015. https://www.kidzworld.com/article/130-cara-beth
-burnside-biogrpahy.

Leonard, Tod. "Skater's MegaRamp is 'Dreamland' for Pros."
    San Diego Union-Tribune, May 31, 2016. https://www
    .sandiegouniontribune.com/sports/sdut-x-games-bob
    -burnquist-megaramp-2016may31-story.html.
National Safety Council. "Skateboarding Safety." Retrieved
    February 25, 2019. https://www.nsc.org/home-safety
    /safety-topics/child-safety/skateboards.
Warin, Robbie. "Pro Legend Tony Trujillo on a Life
    Embedded in Skate Culture." *Huck*, July 11, 2018.
    https://www.huckmag.com/outdoor/skate/skateboard
    -interview-vans-tnt-prototype-tony-trujillo.

INDEX

A

aerial, 13, 33
Armanto, Lizzie, 36–37

B

ban, 7, 9
base plate, 15
beginner, 4, 12, 14, 16, 21,
    23–24
Biniak, Bob, 9
Bones Brigade, 32, 34
Burnquist, Bob, 6, 38
Burnside, Cara-Beth, 36

C

competition, 4, 11, 13, 14, 21, 27,
    30, 32, 36
cruising, 17–18, 23–24
culture, 6–7, 10, 33–34

D

deck, 12, 15, 17–18, 20
do-it-yourself (DIY) culture, 7, 9
downhill skating, 13, 17–18
dropping in, 24

F

falling, 16, 22, 28, 30–31, 37
flip, 24, 26, 34
freestyle skating, 10, 12, 34

G

gear, 5, 12, 14–15, 16, 29, 30
Gelfand, Alan, 10
goofy, 22
grind, 10, 12, 24, 30
grip tape, 20

H

half-pipe, 13, 24
hanger, 18
Hawk, Tony, 6, 32–34
helmet, 12, 18–19, 21, 28–29
hubba, 38

I

injuries, 18–19, 21, 23, 27–28,
    30, 37

K

kickflip, 23, 34
kickturn, 24

L

laws, 9, 30
longboard, 16–18

M

Mullen, Rodney, 10, 12, 31, 34–35

N

Nasworthy, Frank, 11
nose, 15, 17, 22, 26

O

ollie, 4, 10, 12, 24, 25–26, 30, 34

P

padding, 12, 18–20, 21, 27–29
park skating, 13, 17–18
polyurethane, 11
pool, 9–10, 12–13, 18, 24
practice, 6, 9, 12, 16, 21, 24–25,
    32, 36, 38
pumping, 24

Q

quarter-pipe, 13, 24

R

ramp, 10–13, 24, 27, 33–34, 38

S

safety, 14, 21, 27, 29, 30
selling out, 35
shaped decks, 18
shoes, 19–20, 36
short board, 15–16
skate parks, 4–5, 9, 21, 38
skate shops, 7, 9, 14, 17–18, 22, 37

slalom, 13, 17–18
slide, 10, 12
stance, 22–23
street skating, 10, 12–13, 17–18,
    24, 34–35, 38
stretching, 21, 30
surfing, 4, 6–7, 9, 11, 23

T

Thrasher, 10, 36
trick, 4, 9–10, 12–13, 14–16, 18, 20,
    23–26, 27, 30–31, 33–34, 37
trucks, 15, 18, 23, 25, 29
Trujillo, Tony, 33–34
turning, 15–16, 23–26

V

vert, 11–13, 18, 23, 24, 33, 36, 38
video game, 33
videos, 30, 34

W

Weaver, Gregg, 11
wheels, 7, 11, 15–16, 18, 24, 25

X

X Games, 11, 33

Z

Z-Boys, 7, 9

ABOUT THE AUTHOR

Philip Wolny is an editor and author hailing from Poland by way of Queens, New York. He has written extensively for the young adult and teen audience, including books on sports, including several skateboarding-related titles. He lives in New York City with his wife and daughter.

PHOTO CREDITS